LAND OF THE FREE

THE RIGHT TO SPEAK OUT

By
David C. King

THE MILLBROOK PRESS
Brookfield, Connecticut

Published by The Millbrook Press, Inc.
2 Old New Milford Road
Brookfield, CT 06804
© 1997 Blackbirch Graphics, Inc.

5 4 3 2 1

Created and produced in association with Blackbirch Graphics.
Series Editor: Tanya Lee Stone
Editor: Lisa Clyde Nielsen
Associate Editor: Elizabeth M. Taylor
Production Editor: Laura Specht Patchkofsky

Photo credits
Cover and page 6: Photodisc; p. 5: ©Blackbirch Press, Inc.; pp. 8, 9: North
Wind Picture Archives; pp. 12, 42: Collection of the Supreme Court of the
United States; p. 13: Roy Roper/Gamma Liaison; pp. 15, 33: Brad
Markel/Liaison USA; p. 16: ©John A. Giordano/SABA; pp. 18, 41: National
Portrait Gallery; pp. 21, 24, 26: AP/Wide World Photos, Inc.; p. 22:
©Gamma Liaison; p. 25: Pember/The Cincinnati Enquirer/Gamma Liaison;
p. 28: ©Jon Levy/Gamma Liaison; p. 31: ©T. Crosby/Liaison USA; p. 34:
©Susan Greenwood/Gamma Liaison; p. 36: ©Mark Peterson/SABA; p. 38:
©Stephen Perry/Gamma Liaison.

Library of Congress Cataloging-in-Publication Data

King, David C.
The right to speak out / David C. King.
p.   cm. — (Land of the free)
Includes bibliographical references and index.
Summary: Focuses on freedom of speech and of the press while
discussing freedom of expression as guaranteed by the Bill of Rights.
ISBN 0-7613-0063-5 (lib. bdg.)
1. Freedom of speech—United States—Popular works. 2. Freedom
of the press—United States—Popular works.
[1. Freedom of speech. 2. Freedom of the press.] I. Title.
II. Series: Land of the free (Brookfield, Conn.)
KF4772.Z9K56 1997
342.73'0853—dc20
[347.302853] 96-21966 CIP AC

Contents

★ ★ ★ ★ ★ ★

Introduction

★ ★ ★ ★ ★ ★ ★ ★ ★ ★

Suppose that you could be arrested for reading a book, going to church, or talking with your friends. Sound impossible? Not everywhere. Your rights to do all these things, and many others, are guaranteed under U.S. law. But people in many other countries have no such guarantees. Their governments tell them what they may and may not read, write, and say, what religion they must follow, and even how they should vote—that is, if they are allowed to vote at all.

Americans are proud of their freedoms. Even so, many Americans don't know very much about those freedoms, or about the responsibilities that come with them. It is important to understand your rights, so that you can use them—and defend them.

The books in the *Land of the Free* series tell you about our most important American rights and freedoms: the right to speak freely, to vote in elections, to worship as we choose, and to join with others who share our views and goals. Most of these rights are set out in the U.S. Constitution and its first ten amendments, the Bill of Rights.

The Constitution and the Bill of Rights were written more than 200 years ago, soon after the United States won its independence from Britain. The authors of the Constitution believed that freedom would flourish under democracy. A democratic government, elected by the

people, serves the people—not the other way around. Many of the rights in the Constitution help guarantee that democracy will continue.

The authors of the Constitution broke new ground, creating a society that valued and respected liberty. Over the years, adapting to changes in society, Americans have re-interpreted and expanded the rights that the country's founders set out. Yet, the basic principles behind those rights have not changed, and they apply just as well today as they did 200 years ago. Only if we understand how our freedoms work, and why they are essential, will they continue to flourish for years to come.

• Freedom of expression is a basic right for all Americans.

Chapter 1

FREE EXPRESSION IN A FREE SOCIETY

"Congress shall make no law...abridging [restricting] the freedom of speech, or of the press...."

In those few words, the First Amendment to the Constitution of the United States grants one of the most important rights enjoyed by the American people. The right to express one's thoughts and ideas is at the very core of our democratic system of government—that is, a government that is run by the people. In fact, most people believe that without this freedom of expression, democracy cannot really exist.

What exactly does the First Amendment mean? People sometimes remark, "This is a free country, and that means I can say or write anything I want to." At first glance, that is what the words of the First Amendment seem to mean. But did the framers of the Constitution mean that anything people might say or print is protected by the amendment? Or are there times when expression

is illegal? How do we know which forms of expression are illegal? And who decides?

These are the questions we will try to answer in this book. They are questions that help to show us how our democracy works.

Establishing the Right of Free Expression

Our right to express ideas freely grew out of the long struggle for democracy in both England and America. For centuries, it had been a crime to criticize the government of England and the king or queen. When England established its thirteen American colonies, those same strict rules applied. Printers had to answer to the government. Officials, called censors, could destroy or ban publications they did not approve of. They were also allowed to evaluate materials before they were printed and to censor what they did not approve of—a practice that was called prior restraint. Some people who challenged the censors were put in prison, their books were burned, or their printing presses were smashed.

In colonial America, printing presses were often censored by the government.

In the 1600s, some Americans dared to argue that censorship was wrong. They insisted that citizens had certain rights, even against powerful kings and queens. These ideas slowly took hold and, by 1700, the English government ended the practice of prior restraint. But the government kept the right to punish people who criticized it.

An important milestone on the road to freedom of expression was reached in the American colonies in 1735. On a hot August day, a crowd jammed into a courtroom in the colony of New York for the trial of a newspaper publisher named John Peter Zenger.

Zenger's newspaper had printed articles harshly criticizing the governor of New York, a man appointed by the king of England. The furious governor had all copies of the newspaper burned, and Zenger was thrown into prison to await trial.

Copies of Zenger's *Weekly Journal* were burned after the newspaper criticized the governor.

Nearly everyone in the courtroom expected the jury to find Zenger guilty. But Zenger's lawyer, Andrew Hamilton, presented a brilliant argument. What counted, Hamilton said, was whether the statements in the newspaper were true or false. Thus, if Zenger had printed lies, then he deserved to be punished. But if he printed the truth, Zenger should go free, because the people had a right to know the truth about their own government.

This case, Hamilton concluded, involved more than John Peter Zenger. Instead, it was a trial about liberty, the liberty of "speaking and writing truth."

In a matter of minutes, the jury returned the verdict: "Not guilty." As the crowd cheered Zenger's freedom, an important idea was taking shape in the minds of the colonists—the idea that the press should always be free to print the truth.

About 30 years after the Zenger trial, the colonists began the struggle for independence from English rule. This struggle would lead to the Declaration of Independence and the American Revolution. During these years of conflict, the colonists relied on sharing their grievances against the English government and the king. The colonies formed "Committees of Correspondence" to exchange information. And even though English authorities continued to arrest some printers, the colonists used newspapers and pamphlets to spread ideas. By daring to speak and write about what actions to take against the British, the colonies established the unity they needed to declare and win their independence.

The American people knew that their insistence on free expression was vital to the cause of independence. As soon as independence was declared, each of the thirteen colonies became a state and wrote a state constitution. Most of these constitutions included a "bill of rights," a document that guaranteed such liberties as freedom of expression. In 1787, when the U.S. Constitution was written, people wanted to be sure that individual rights were protected from the national government as well. The specific protections Americans wanted were written into the Bill of Rights, which contained the first ten

Thomas Paine and the Power of a Free Press

By the year 1775, the American colonists were at war with England, but they were not sure how far to go in this struggle for their rights. Many colonists felt that they were still English subjects. They were not ready to cut all ties with England by declaring independence.

Then, early in 1776, a newcomer to America named Thomas Paine published a pamphlet called *Common Sense*. In simple but powerful language, Paine argued that it was "common sense" for the thirteen colonies to declare independence and form a new nation. More than 150,000 copies of Paine's pamphlet were sold in just a few months. His arguments helped to convince many Americans that they should be fighting for their independence.

On July 4, 1776, the Declaration of Independence was issued by the Continental Congress. Paine's freedom to print his ideas had helped Americans make one of the most important decisions in our history.

amendments to the Constitution. The Bill of Rights became part of the Constitution in 1791.

The main reason for writing freedom of expression into the First Amendment was to guarantee that the people would always be free to discuss and write about matters of government.

Many years later, Oliver Wendell Holmes, Jr., a famous justice of the Supreme Court, called our democracy a "marketplace of ideas." By this he meant that people must be free to hear a variety of ideas. They can accept, or "buy," the best ideas, and discard others. "The best test of truth," Holmes wrote in 1920, "is the power of the

Supreme Court Justice Oliver Wendell Holmes believed that, in a free society, the "market" would naturally accept good ideas and reject bad ones.

[idea] to get itself accepted in the competition of the market....That...is the theory of our Constitution."

A Freedom with Limits

The First Amendment states our basic right to freedom of expression. But does that mean complete freedom in every situation?

The framers of the Constitution recognized that there might need to be limits on what people were free to say or write. What was not clear—and is still not clear today—is what those limits were and who would decide.

The second question was easier to answer than the first. The nation's courts, especially the Supreme Court, have the task of deciding how the First Amendment should be applied to particular situations. In 1925, for example, the nine justices of the Supreme Court made an important decision in a case involving a man named Benjamin Gitlow, who had been arrested under a state law for criticizing the government. In making a decision in the case, the justices ruled that freedom of expression is so important that it must be protected from state governments as well as from the federal government.

When the Supreme Court makes a ruling like this, it is called a landmark decision. The decision guides the lower courts in the country on similar future cases. A landmark decision tells the courts how the Supreme Court is currently applying the First Amendment to certain situations. Following the landmark decision in the Gitlow case, the Supreme Court continued to apply the First Amendment to both state and national laws.

The other question—What are the limits of free expression?—is much more difficult to answer. In fact, courts have been wrestling with that question for more

Sometimes freedom of expression allows people to express hate, such as in this demonstration by the Ku Klux Klan.

than 200 years. Here are some of the reasons it is so hard to tell exactly what freedom of expression means:

1. *Conflict with other rights.* Sometimes the right of freedom of expression can conflict with another right. Freedom of the press, for example, enables someone to criticize a government official. But what happens if a reporter's news story unfairly hurts an official's reputation? The courts have to protect the freedom of the press—but they also have to protect individuals from vicious and false attacks.

A similar conflict might come up in a criminal court case, such as a murder trial involving a famous person. People are eager to hear the full story. But what happens if some news reports convince people that the defendant is guilty, even before the case goes to a jury? The defendant has a right to a fair trial. The courts must decide if press coverage has interfered with that right.

2. *Hate speech.* Some people use freedom of expression to deliver ugly messages of hate against other individuals or groups. Members of the Ku Klux Klan (KKK), for instance, have often said and printed vicious things about African Americans. In much the same way, members of the American Nazi party have delivered messages of hate against Jews, immigrants, and other groups. Should such statements of hate be allowed? Or should the government pass laws to prohibit hate speech in order to protect the targets of those expressions?

3. *The nation's security.* While people do have the right to speak out against the government, this can cause problems in time of war or any other national emergency.

Should people be allowed to present news of government activities that might jeopardize our nation? Or does the government have the right to silence people in order to protect the nation's security?

The American people debate all of these issues with great care. Most believe that there must be some limits to freedom of speech and of the press. But they insist that any such limits be very narrow and clearly defined in order to protect a right that is so fundamental to the health of our democracy.

During the Gulf War, there was debate over whether news coverage might compromise national security.

• Free speech can include forms of symbolic expression,
such as burning the American flag.

Chapter 2

WHAT ARE THE LIMITS OF FREE EXPRESSION?

The Constitution, with the Bill of Rights added in 1791, established the United States as the most democratic nation in the world. Freedom of expression, along with other personal liberties, was now part of the law of the land. However, no one knew yet what kinds of expression would not be protected by the First Amendment. In other words, people did not know what would happen if Congress did pass a law "abridging the freedom of speech, or of the press." Those matters could be decided only by experience as the nation began its great experiment in democracy.

The Question of National Security

One of the first, and most important, issues that Americans faced was whether the government could limit freedom of expression in order to protect the nation's security. The issue was not

presented to the Supreme Court until 1919—more than a century after the First Amendment was added to the Constitution.

Twice before, the U.S. government had placed severe limits on freedom of expression in the name of protecting the nation. First, in 1798, during a conflict with France, Congress passed the Sedition Act, a law making it a crime to speak or write anything that would harm the reputation of the Congress or the president. The second instance came during the Civil War (1861–1865), when President Abraham Lincoln used his emergency powers to have several newspapers shut down because they opposed his policies.

In both these cases, many Americans were angered by the government's actions. How could democracy work, they asked, if people were not free to criticize the government? In 1798, Thomas Jefferson said that the Sedition Act made him "afraid to write what I think." And during the Civil War, a furious newspaper editor demanded, "By whom and when was Abraham Lincoln made dictator [an absolute ruler] of this country?"

Had the government gone too far in trying to silence its critics? The question was not really answered in either of those instances, because no Supreme Court case challenged the government's authority.

Government leaders—such as President Lincoln—have sometimes felt it necessary to limit freedom of expression to protect the country.

The issue finally reached the Supreme Court nearly 55 years later, in cases resulting from government actions during World War I. When America entered that conflict in 1917, most Americans eagerly supported the war effort. But a small minority was bitterly opposed. The protestors gave speeches and wrote pamphlets denouncing the government and urging young men to resist the draft, which required them to serve in the military. To stop these critics, Congress passed another Sedition Act. This new law prohibited "disloyal, profane...or abusive" speech or writing about the government, the Constitution, the American flag, or the armed forces. More than 900 people were imprisoned due to the Sedition Act.

This time, the government's actions were challenged in cases that reached the Supreme Court in 1919. The protestors claimed that the Sedition Act was unconstitutional because it violated their First Amendment right to freedom of expression. But the justices of the Court voted unanimously in *Schenck* v. *The United States of America* that the Sedition Act was indeed constitutional and did not violate anyone's rights. Justice Oliver Wendell Holmes, Jr., explained that "in ordinary times, [the protestors] would have been within their constitutional rights" to oppose government actions. But, he said, wartime was different. If any speech or writing presents a "clear and present danger" to the country, then Congress has the right to pass laws to prevent it.

In his written opinion, the justice explained in more detail what he meant by a "clear and present danger." Justice Holmes intended the decision to cover instances

where language or expression could incite violence or cause harm to others. If someone falsely shouted "Fire!" in a crowded theater and caused a panic, that person would not be protected by the First Amendment. The false cry of "Fire!" would create a "clear and present danger" for the people in the theater because it would cause them to act in a way that could potentially harm them. In the same way, if a speech or a piece of writing causes people to act in a way that would threaten the nation's safety, or might result in violence, then the government can act to protect the nation or public safety.

Since 1919, the Supreme Court has turned to the idea of "clear and present danger" many times. In the 1940s and 1950s, for example, the Court upheld laws against members of the Communist party, because Communists spoke in favor of a revolution that would lead to "the violent overthrow of the government."

More recently, however, the justices have sometimes found it hard to decide when expressions actually present a clear and present danger to the nation or to public safety. In 1969, the Supreme Court heard a case involving a Ku Klux Klan leader who had been convicted under a state law for saying he was in favor of using violence against African Americans. The Court overturned his conviction because, the justices said, the speech had not created any "immediate" threat of violence.

In all of these cases, the Supreme Court has tried to find a balance between the individual's right to free expression and the government's duty to protect the nation or prevent violence. Since the 1969 case involving the KKK

In the image, the map is titled: COMMUNIST PARTY ORGANIZATION U.S.A–FEB. 9, 1950

leader, the Court has said that the government must prove that speech or writing presents a real and serious threat to the country's safety. Otherwise, the justices have said, it is too easy to say that any criticism of the government or talk of violence is a danger and must be silenced. While members of the Communist party were jailed in the 1940s, they would not be jailed today. As a result of the 1969 case, the Court today would not uphold laws prohibiting Communists from talking about the need for a revolution—unless they were urging people to actually take up arms and start fighting.

In the 1950s, Senator Joseph McCarthy led a movement that infringed upon people's right to belong to the Communist party.

Protecting a Person's Reputation

Another area in which laws have been passed limiting freedom of expression involves words that defame, or injure, a person's reputation. Printed words that hurt someone's reputation, or hold them up to ridicule, are called libel. If the defaming words are spoken instead of printed, it is a case of slander. False statements are usually at the core of slander and libel cases.

An individual who feels wronged can sue in court, and can win money "damages." In these cases, the courts weigh the right of freedom of expression against the person's right to be protected from vicious and false accusations.

Celebrities bear the burden of proving that statements printed about them are false in order to win a libel suit.

Court cases dealing with libel often involve news reports about a government official or a famous person. In 1964, the Supreme Court ruled that criticism of a government official is libel only if the wronged person can prove that the statements were false and were made with malice—that is, if the person who made the statement knew it was false. Later, the same standard was extended to "public figures," such as celebrities. Some people have criticized this standard, arguing that it places too much of a burden on the person who feels wronged. This, they say, is why the tabloids, or "scandal sheets," can print outrageous stories about famous people. The publishers know it would be hard to prove libel.

Supporters of the Supreme Court ruling argue that if it is too easy to prove libel or slander, then reporters may be afraid to criticize anyone for fear of being taken to court. This fear of libel suits, they say, would be as bad as censorship and would deprive people of their right to know the truth about the nation's public figures.

Freedom of the Press and Censorship

In countries that are ruled by dictators, the government controls speech and press through censorship. Government censors decide exactly what information the public will be allowed to receive, and when.

Americans have always been strongly opposed to censorship. They believe that any limits on freedom of expression should be applied and judged after the expression is made public, not before.

President Nixon tried—and failed—to block publication of "The Pentagon Papers" in 1971.

Are there times, however, when the government should step in and stop a publication, a movie, or a television program before it is released to the public? President Richard M. Nixon believed that such a time had come in 1971, when two newspapers planned to print documents known as "The Pentagon Papers." The documents, which had been stolen from government offices, told of government actions during the Vietnam War. Government lawyers argued that publishing the papers would be harmful to the security of the United States.

The Supreme Court ruled against the president and allowed the papers to be published. The justices decided that, although the documents might embarrass the government, they did not endanger the nation. Justice Hugo L. Black wrote, "The press must be left free to publish the news, whatever the sources, without censorship...or prior restraint."

One area where limited censorship has been allowed involves obscenity—expressions that include profanity or material that most people would find vulgar or offensive. State and local governments have passed many laws to prohibit obscenity in publications and movies, especially for the protection of children. The Supreme Court has

often upheld these laws, as long as they do not restrict material that has literary, artistic, or other merit.

Some of the laws have presented the Court with its most difficult cases. Since 1957, more than 20 cases have reached the Supreme Court challenging state or local obscenity laws as unconstitutional. The main problem that the justices have faced is deciding *what* material is offensive, and *who* should decide if material is offensive. If some people in the community, or a state, object to a movie, for example, should everyone be denied the liberty of viewing that film? So far, no one has come up with a definition of obscenity that can be applied to all cases.

In 1990, Cincinnati, Ohio, was divided over an art exhibit that featured homo-sexuality and violence. Some material was censored, caus-ing a public outcry.

In the 1960s and 1970s, demonstrators burned draft cards to protest the Vietnam War.

Speech Without Words

During the Vietnam War, a young man decided to protest the war by publicly burning his draft card (which required him to register for military service). And another young man showed his opposition to the war by standing on a street corner and burning an American flag. Both protestors were arrested, tried, and convicted—found guilty.

And both appealed their convictions through the lower courts all the way to the Supreme Court.

The two men claimed that their arrests violated their right to freedom of speech. The Court had to decide two questions: First, were the protestors' actions a form of speech, even though no words were used? And, second, if these actions were speech, were they protected by the First Amendment?

The Supreme Court ruled that both burning a draft card and burning an American flag were forms of symbolic speech. That means that actions or symbols are a form of expression, even without words. In the case of the flag burner, the justices voted five to four that the man had a right under the Constitution to express his opinion about the flag by setting it on fire. But in the draft card case, the young man's conviction was upheld. The justices ruled that burning a draft card interfered with the government's right to raise a military force.

In facing such issues, the Supreme Court has tried to protect every American's right to freedom of expression. A limit on that freedom is allowed just in those cases where it can be proved that this is the only way to protect another, perhaps even more important, right such as the security of the nation, or public safety.

Some people feel that the Supreme Court has sometimes gone too far in protecting freedom of expression. This sometimes occurs when people object to unpopular expression. Other people, however, believe that the Supreme Court goes too far in *limiting* freedom of expression, especially in upholding obscenity laws.

• Freedom of expression continues to be challenged in modern society. Singer Sister Souljah's violent lyrics, for example, have caused controversy.

Chapter 3

THE CONTINUING DEBATE

Americans today still wrestle with new areas of freedom of expression. One reason for the ongoing debate is that modern technology—especially computers—has produced whole new areas of expression. With cable and satellite television, along with computer networks, millions of words and pictures can be brought directly into America's homes. The power of this technology worries many.

Another great change in our society over the past several decades has been in attitudes about what is considered offensive. Expressions that would not have been allowed in earlier times are now acceptable to most Americans. For instance, in the 1939 movie *Gone With the Wind*, actor Clark Gable spoke the line, "Frankly...I don't give a damn!" At the time, many viewers were shocked by the use of the word "damn" in a film; today, that language is considered mild.

The Flag Burning Debate Continues

Many people were outraged by the Supreme Court ruling that burning an American flag was a constitutional use of free speech. Congress responded to the public outcry in 1989 by passing a law called the Flag Protection Act. The new law made it a crime to knowingly mutilate or destroy the national flag. But when the law was challenged in 1990, the Supreme Court ruled that the Flag Protection Act violated principles of the First Amendment. Burning the American flag, the justices said, was a statement of a political position that did not interfere with the rights of others or threaten the nation's security. Some members of Congress have recently proposed an amendment to the Constitution as their final attempt to outlaw the burning of the American flag.

As our society's standards have changed, many Americans have come to feel that there should be no limits on free expression. But others are convinced that freedom of expression has gone too far, and that this cherished right is being abused. They argue that the content of some movies, television programs, publications, and popular music has gone far beyond the bounds of decency. There is a fear that our society's values and moral standards are being damaged.

As in the past, the American people and the courts are trying to find a balance between freedom of expression and the well-being of our society. But the great changes of the past half-century have made it more and more difficult to find that balance.

Freedom in the Computer Age

The "information superhighway" has changed global communication. From their homes, people can gain access to publications from all over the world. To write a school paper, a student who goes "on-line" can find far more information than Thomas Jefferson had in his entire library in the early 1800s. Much of this information flows through the Internet and World Wide Web, which link together thousands of communications services.

As happens with other forms of expression, some people use this technology to create material that is hate-filled, violent, or offensive. In 1994, for instance, a college student published a story on the Internet about the brutal murder of a woman. Although his story was fiction, he used the name of a real person, so police

Parents and teachers are eager to train children to use computers, but some are wary of the material that computer users can access.

arrested him for publishing a threat to injure the woman. The case against him was dismissed, however. The judge ruled that the story was ugly and violent, but it did not represent a real danger to anyone.

Many people are troubled that this kind of material can flow freely on the Internet. They are especially concerned that parents have no way of knowing what their children are being exposed to on home computers. Others believe it is the parents' responsibility, not the government's, to monitor what their kids are doing.

In 1995, the Senate tried to calm these fears with a bill called the Communications Decency Act. The bill sought to make it a crime to put "hateful or indecent" material on the Internet. The bill, however, faced strong opposition in the House of Representatives and among the public. Many people worried that the plan could lead to government censors deciding what is "hateful or indecent." Even without government censors, the fear of being arrested would make people reluctant to enter on the Internet any information that might offend someone. The critics also argued that it would be wrong to hamper the free flow of information simply because a tiny percentage of users might abuse the freedom.

There is also the legal question of whether controlling messages on the Internet would be constitutional. The Supreme Court has not yet ruled on whether computer-based networks like the Internet are a form of print, like books and magazines, or a form of broadcasting, like radio and television. Print materials are subject to very few federal government controls. Broadcasting, however,

is regulated by a government agency that can prohibit certain forms of expression, such as using vulgar language on radio or television programs.

Most Americans agree that computer users, especially parents of young children, need some way to monitor what kind of material is coming into their homes. More than 80 percent of people surveyed, however, are also opposed to government controls.

The communications industry itself is now trying to address these growing concerns. In 1995, a committee representing most of the computer on-line services began developing codes that will let computer users know what materials contain violence or might be offensive in other ways. Parents will then be able to use a special computer chip, called the V-chip, to block coded material that

President Clinton, with Vice-President and Mrs. Gore, holds a V-chip that censors materials on television.

might be upsetting to children or other household members. A similar "parental lock" is already used for cable and satellite television sets.

Vulgar Words and Violent Messages

One area in which many people feel that freedom of expression is being abused is in popular music, especially rap songs, or hip-hop. The songs of Trent Reznor and the group Nine Inch Nails, for example, have outraged people because they deal with such subjects as murder, suicide, and insanity. Critics say that such lyrics are especially harmful to children. Some rap artists also use their CDs or tapes to deliver what some feel are messages of anger and hate. Others believe this is legitimate political expression. Many people were upset by a 1992 rap song by Sister Souljah, which declared that African Americans had been killing one another long enough, and the time had come to start killing white people.

Although many Americans are offended by such lyrics, few arrests or court cases have resulted from them.

Rap singer Luther "Skyywalker" Campbell was one target of censorship campaigns.

In 1990, rap artist Luther "Skyywalker" Campbell of 2 Live Crew was arrested after a concert in Florida on the charge that the lyrics of one song violated local obscenity laws. The jury quickly found Campbell "Not guilty." One juror explained that the lyrics were no worse than those of dozens of other rap songs, so it would have been unfair to convict Campbell.

If most Americans are deeply offended by vulgar words and messages of violence or hate, why shouldn't laws be passed to prohibit them? Justices of the Supreme Court attempt to explain why it is so important to protect all forms of expression, even messages that are as upsetting as those contained in some rap songs. In one case, for example, the Court overturned the conviction of a man who had made a vicious, hate-filled speech about American Jews. The Court's majority opinion explained that "...a function of free speech under our system of government is to invite dispute. It may indeed best serve its high purpose when it [leads to] unrest, creates dissatisfaction with conditions as they are, or even stirs people to anger." In this way, the Court believed that, to keep our democracy working as a "marketplace of ideas," we must protect everyone's right to speak out—even when we do not like what they say.

Commercial Speech

Advertising is a form of expression that is protected by the First Amendment; however, courts have given it less protection than other types of speech. This includes ads in magazines and newspapers, signs and billboards, and

Cigarette ads often portray smoking as part of having fun. Critics worry that these ads are aimed at young people.

the commercials on radio and television. How much protection should "commercial speech" enjoy? The debate has been heated, particularly over advertising by cigarette companies.

Every day of the year, an average of 3,000 teenagers begin smoking cigarettes, and for many, this will lead to a dangerous lifelong habit. Most Americans believe that cigarette advertising contributes to the problem by luring young people into smoking. Many believe that the ads create the idea that smoking is a way to show that you are popular or tough or cool. Over the past 30 years, there has been growing pressure on the government to ban all advertising by tobacco companies.

The first step was taken when the Federal Communications Commission (FCC), the government agency that

controls broadcasting, announced in 1971 that cigarette commercials would no longer be allowed on television or radio. At the same time, the government required that all cigarette ads in newspapers and magazines include a warning about the health risks of smoking cigarettes.

In 1995, President Bill Clinton announced the next step in the effort to shield young people from the power of cigarette advertisements. He ordered a government agency to draw up regulations that would include a ban on cigarette billboards near schools and playgrounds. New restrictions on magazine and newspaper ads were also planned.

The tobacco companies, however, insist that the new regulations will violate their First Amendment guarantee of freedom of expression. Their spokespersons say that the president's plan is a step toward outlawing all cigarette advertising. Five tobacco companies announced plans to file a lawsuit to see if the new regulations are constitutional. Once again, the courts will try to find a balance between freedom of expression and the government's efforts to protect young Americans.

As these issues show, there is no final answer to the many questions about freedom of expression and its limits. Most Americans today are even more strongly opposed to government interference than were their parents or grandparents. Yet many people are concerned about the amount of vulgarity, violence, and other possibly offensive material produced in today's media. Their greatest worry is that today's young people may become confused about society's values and codes of conduct.

• Often, groups who share a common cause or goal use their rights of freedom of expression (and assembly) to vocalize their beliefs.

Chapter 4

WHAT DOES FREEDOM OF EXPRESSION MEAN TO YOU?

The First Amendment guarantees freedom of expression to every person in the nation. Does it apply to children under age 18 as well? No one was certain about this until actual situations arose involving young Americans' freedom of speech and of the press.

The question did not reach the Supreme Court until the 1960s. During the Vietnam War, four Iowa teenagers decided to state their opposition to the war by wearing black armbands to school. School officials had issued a warning that anyone wearing the armbands in school would be suspended, but the teens went ahead with their protest.

When the students were suspended, two of them, Mary Beth Tinker and her brother, John, appealed to the courts. After losing in the lower courts, the Tinkers won their case before the Supreme Court in 1969. The justices ruled that the wearing of

the armbands had not interfered with other students' rights, so the four should not have been suspended. "Students in school as well as out of school," the decision stated, "are persons under our Constitution."

The Tinker case suggests that young people do have constitutional rights to free expression. But the Supreme Court has also made it clear that there are some situations in which the right can be limited. This is especially true where the protection of children is involved.

Protecting Children

Like America's adults, young people have the right of free expression as long as it does not interfere with the rights of others. School represents a special situation; it is the place where all young people have the right to learn. If a student speaks or acts in a way that disrupts a class, or interferes with another student's right to learn, that is not a lawful use of free expression.

Similar conditions apply to students' freedom of the press in school newspapers and other writing. Young people do have freedom of the press, but their words or pictures cannot interfere with the main purpose of the school. This means that the teacher-adviser on a school paper can censor students' work—but only if it is felt that the material will disrupt the school. These areas are still a bit unclear, however, and courts continue to evaluate specific cases one by one.

In the interest of protecting children, some communities have been able to ban certain books from libraries and to prohibit their use in classrooms. The idea behind

banning books is to keep young people from being exposed to too much violence, or to language or ideas that are considered offensive.

But many people feel that some communities and local schools go too far with this form of censorship. They point out that great works of literature are sometimes banned merely to satisfy a small group that finds the works offensive.

Mark Twain's *Huckleberry Finn*, for example, has been banned in a number of schools because of Twain's description of an escaped slave. Those who ban the book say that the language and ideas might be offensive to young African Americans. The critics of book banning say that the language was commonplace in Twain's day and was not meant to show disrespect. In addition, they argue, it is wrong to deprive students in one school of a great work that is widely read throughout the country, and to ban it to satisfy only one group.

Another argument against book banning is that children are regularly exposed to far more offensive material in movies, television programs, and popular music. Some people also argue that once book banning begins, it becomes easier for people to insist that other works also be prohibited.

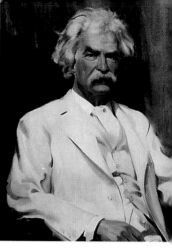

Works by Mark Twain, one of America's greatest writers, have been banned many times.

Citizenship, Not Censorship

Americans enjoy great freedom of expression. Protecting that freedom means respecting the right of others to express themselves. At times, that can be hard to do, because the words or actions of others can make us angry or upset.

It is important to remember, however, that the freedom exists only when it exists for everyone. Justice Oliver Wendell Holmes, Jr., said that freedom of expression means "not only freedom for those who agree with us, but [also] freedom for the thought we hate." This is the great strength of American democracy. The marketplace of ideas works as long as we are willing to be tolerant of all people and all shades of opinion.

But what about forms of expression that people find offensive, such as song lyrics that promote hatred or violence? Many people feel that the best way to combat false or unhealthy messages is with healthy ones. Another great justice of the Supreme Court, Louis Brandeis, said, "The remedy...is more speech, not enforced silence" through government laws or censorship.

Individuals and groups of people have applied this idea to the situations they feel need to be changed. A group of teenagers in Boston, Massachusetts, for example, were upset when a billboard advertising cigarettes was put up near their school. After discussing the matter with their parents, they visited city officials who arranged a meeting with representatives of the tobacco company so the teenagers could voice their opinion. In this case, the company considered their views and made a decision to remove the billboard.

In the late 1700s, the Constitution and the Bill of Rights established the United States as a democratic nation. Over the next 200 years, this American framework of government inspired people throughout the world. As other countries and

Supreme Court Justice Louis Brandeis believed that free expression of all viewpoints was best for society.

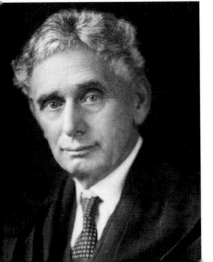

On Freedom of Expression: The Thoughts of Four Presidents

Dwight D. Eisenhower, 1953: "The libraries of America are and must ever remain the home of free, inquiring minds. To them, our citizens—of all ages and races, of all creeds and political persuasions—must ever be able to turn...freely to seek the whole truth."

John F. Kennedy, 1962: "A nation that is afraid to let its people judge the truth and falsehood of ideas in an open market is a nation that is afraid of its people."

Ronald Reagan, 1982: "In the First Amendment to the Constitution, our Founding Fathers affirmed their belief that competing ideas are fundamental to our freedom. We Americans cherish our freedom of expression and our access to multiple sources of news and information."

Bill Clinton, 1994 "[Rather than censorship] what we can call for is corporate responsibility. We can all urge the entertainment industry to consider the impact of their work, and to understand the damage that comes from the incessant, repetitive, mindless violence...that permeates our media all the time."

peoples gained independence from monarchs, dictators, or colonial powers, they often established constitutions with a bill of rights based on the American model.

Our written framework of government has worked for more than two centuries for two main reasons: First, the framers made it flexible enough to meet the needs of changing times. Second, the American people have worked hard to uphold such basic principles as freedom of speech. How well it works in the future depends on the willingness of "We, the people" to apply those principles.

Understanding the Bill of Rights

In 1791, the Bill of Rights became part of the U.S. Constitution. What are these rights and why are they important for us?

The First Amendment says that the government cannot interfere with people's rights to freedom of speech, freedom of the press, freedom of religion, and freedom of assembly. It also gives people the right to petition their leaders.

The Second Amendment says because a "well-regulated militia" is "necessary to the security of a free state," the government can't interfere with the people's right to "keep and bear arms." Arms are guns and other weapons.

At the time the Bill of Rights was written, most men still belonged to their local state militia, or army. They kept their guns at home so they could be ready to defend their country at a moment's notice.

Some people say that because we have no such state militia today, the Second Amendment doesn't give people the right to own guns. But other people say that the Second Amendment guarantees the right to own guns for many purposes, including defense of home and family.

The Third Amendment says that, except in time of war, troops cannot be lodged in private homes without the permission of homeowners. This was included because many people remembered a time when the British had forced citizens to open their homes to soldiers.

The Fourth Amendment says that people's homes and possessions can't be searched or taken without an official paper called a *warrant*. A warrant is a document, signed by a judge, that allows police to search for evidence of a crime. The amendment also says that a warrant cannot be issued without "*probable cause*." This means that the police must convince a judge that the search of a specific place is likely to produce evidence of a crime.

The Fifth Amendment protects people who are accused of crimes. It says that for a serious crime, such as murder, a person must be charged with the crime by a group called a grand jury. Twelve to twenty-three people make up a grand jury. They must examine the evidence that the government has against the person and then determine whether there is a strong enough case to charge the person with a crime.

The Fifth Amendment also says that a person can't be tried twice for the same crime and doesn't have to testify against himself or herself. In a trial, when someone who is on trial refuses to answer questions on the witness stand, we say the witness "takes the fifth."

Another important part of the Fifth Amendment says that no person can be "deprived of life, liberty, or property, without due process of law." This part of the amendment guarantees all citizens the right to a fair trial before they can be executed, put in prison, or have property taken away from them. It also means that any laws made in the United States must result in fair treatment of all citizens.

Last, the Fifth Amendment says that the government can't take anyone's property for public use without paying a fair price for it.

The Sixth Amendment gives people who are accused of crimes the right to a speedy and public trial by a jury of people from the area where the crime was committed. Without the right to a speedy trial, people could be arrested for crimes and stay in jail for years without ever having the chance to defend themselves in court. The amendment also says that those accused of crimes have the right to know their accusers, to be confronted by the people who have accused them, and to have a lawyer defend them.

The Seventh Amendment gives people involved in lawsuits over money or property the right to trial by a jury. It also says that once a decision is made by that jury, the decision can't be changed unless it can be shown that the trial was flawed in some way.

The Eighth Amendment protects people who are put in jail. The first part of the amendment says that a judge cannot require "excessive bail" for someone accused of a crime. Bail is money that a person must pay to be freed from jail during the time before a trial begins. The money is returned after a person shows up for trial.

The Eighth Amendment also says that no one can be given "cruel and unusual punishment" for a crime. If a person were convicted of stealing a loaf of bread, for example, it would be cruel and unusual punishment to sentence that person to ten years in jail. The rule against cruel and unusual punishment also prevents such things as the torture of prisoners.

The Ninth Amendment says that the fact that some rights are not specifically mentioned does not mean that the people do not have them.

The Tenth Amendment says that any powers not given to the government by the Constitution belong to the states and the people. This amendment was very important to people at the time the Bill of Rights was ratified. Many people still feared a large, powerful national government, and this amendment put limits on the government.

The Bill of Rights gave citizens of the United States many freedoms and protections that few people in other parts of the world had.

Glossary

★ ★ ★ ★ ★ ★

censorship Prohibition of the publication or broadcast of material judged to be dangerous to public welfare or offensive to community moral standards. A form of this is called prior restraint.

commercial speech A term that is used to refer to the words and images of advertisements and radio and television commercials.

landmark decision A Supreme Court decision that shows how the nation's highest court is interpreting the Constitution.

libel A false or misleading written statement or picture that harms a person's reputation.

obscenity Material that is considered offensive to a community's standards of decency.

sedition Words or actions intended to stir up rebellion against the government.

Sedition Act In 1798, and again in 1917, Congress passed laws making it a crime to print or speak anything that was so critical of the government that it would give "aid and comfort" to an enemy in wartime. In both 1798 and 1917, the laws created controversy because this was a form of censorship. In 1919, however, the Supreme Court upheld the 1917 Sedition Act.

slander A false or misleading spoken statement that injures a person's reputation.

symbolic speech Actions or symbols that present a message or idea without words.

Further Reading

★ ★ ★ ★ ★ ★ ★ ★ ★ ★ ★ ★

Coleman, Warren. *The Bill of Rights.* Chicago: Children's Press, 1989.

Evans, J. Edward. *Freedom of the Press.* Minneapolis, MN: Lerner, 1990.

————. *Freedom of Speech.* Minneapolis, MN: Lerner, 1990.

Goldish, Meish. *Our Supreme Court.* Brookfield, CT: Millbrook Press, 1994.

Johnson, Linda Carlson. *Our Constitution.* Brookfield, CT: Millbrook Press, 1992.

Index

★ ★ ★ ★